SACRED CRYSTALS

SACRED CRYSTALS

HAZEL RAVEN

STERLING ETHOS
New York

STERLING ETHOS
New York

STERLING ETHOS and the distinctive
Sterling Ethos logo are registered
trademarks of Sterling Publishing Co., Inc.

ISBN 978-1-4549-2887-4

Distributed in Canada by Sterling Publishing Co., Inc.
c/o Canadian Manda Group, 664 Annette Street,
Toronto, Ontario M6S 2C8, Canada

For information about custom editions, special sales,
and premium and corporate purchases, please
contact Sterling Special Sales at 800-805-5489
or specialsales@sterlingpublishing.com.

Manufactured in China

sterlingpublishing.com

Conceived, designed, and produced by
Quarto Publishing
an imprint of The Quarto Group
The Old Brewery,
6 Blundell Street
London N7 9BH
www.quartoknows.com

QUA: CSTL

6 8 10 9 7

MIX
Paper from
responsible sources
FSC® C016973

CONTENTS

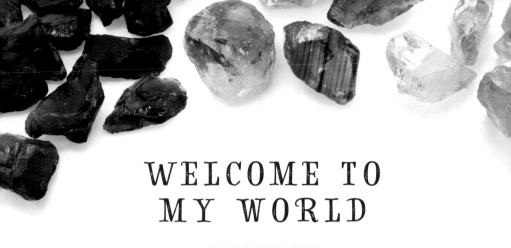

WELCOME TO MY WORLD

Hello, my name is Hazel Raven. I first became interested in crystals in 1989, during a yoga meditation session. Although at that time there was very little information available on crystal healing, I was driven to devote all my energies to exploring the magical world of crystals. I mostly used my intuition, but I also researched and studied gemology and geology.

Since that day all those years ago, I have never looked back, because crystals and promoting crystal healing has become my life's work. As a trainer of professional crystal therapists worldwide for more than 26 years, I have seen the positive effects of crystal healing many times over. I have given lectures worldwide at crystal conferences to many thousands of people, and presented crystal therapy workshops on three continents.

•

Throughout my life I have been fascinated by complementary medicine and the development of higher consciousness through personal growth. This has inspired me to create my own unique style of healing that combines the energies of crystals, color, sacred sounds, chakras, angels, and gemstone essences. These essences focus on maintaining a healthy flow of energy, ensuring the chakras are open, clear, and rotating correctly.

•

You will discover that the colored photographs of the crystals in this book bring an immediate energetic link to the stones. Through these images, you can create a resonant connection with the stone itself and, with practice, you can learn to derive therapeutic benefits.

ABOUT
CRYSTALS

THE HEALING POWER OF CRYSTALS

CRYSTALS AND GEMSTONES HAVE BEEN USED FOR THOUSANDS OF
YEARS FOR DECORATION, PHYSICAL ADORNMENT, HEALING,
PROTECTION, MAGIC, AND RELIGIOUS CEREMONIES.

CRYSTAL CHARACTERISTICS

Crystals are the most organized and stable examples
of physical matter in the natural world, and represent
the lowest state of entropy (disorder) possible. All
crystalline structures are made up of mathematically
precise arrangements of atoms. This is the crystalline
lattice, which confers a high level of stability. It also gives
crystals their unique colors, hardness, geometrical shapes,
and subtle energy properties.

NATURAL ENERGY RESONATORS

Crystals have a remarkable capacity to absorb, store, reflect,
and radiate light in the form of intelligent fields of stable
energy that increase the flow of vital life-force within the
human body, chakras, aura, and other subtle energy
systems. By applying this constant energy, or crystal
resonance, in a coherent, focused way to dysfunctional
energy systems, they restore balance and stability.

This ancient Australian
aboriginal spearhead is flecked
with smoky quartz for luck.

HEALING METHODS

The use of gemstones as jewelry dates back at least to the Paleolithic age. Perhaps the first written accounts of crystal healing came from the ancient Egyptians, who gave detailed recipes for using gemstones such as malachite. We still have written knowledge of the Ayurvedic and Tantric scholars who knew the potential of precious stones. Crystals were prescribed as protection from negative planetary influences, and either worn as jewelry or taken orally as pates or oxides to influence the aura, as well as working through the nervous, lymphatic, and nadis systems (channels through which the cosmic energy prana flows).

•

Modern crystal healers initially focused very much on the properties of clear quartz, but over the last 30 years many people have begun working with the ancient art of the "laying on of stones," especially the placement of crystals on the chakras. Crystals and gemstones help to realign, rebalance, and energize the chakras into appropriate functions.

This scarab pectoral from the tomb of Tutankhamen is made from gold inlaid with lapis lazuli, amber, and other precious stones.

Modern crystal healers place stones in corresponding colors onto the chakras of the body.

HEALING THE CHAKRAS

Balancing the chakras is at the heart of modern crystal healing. The seven major chakras lie in the center line of the body. These funnel-shaped vortexes of energy absorb and distribute life-force or qi. The position of the chakras corresponds to the positions and functions of the glands of the endocrine system and the positions of the nerve ganglia along the spinal column. Well-functioning chakras are believed to vibrate at the frequency of one of the colors of the rainbow spectrum.

CROWN

Position: Just above the top of the head

Color: Violet or clear

Malfunctions: Headaches, nightmares, eye problems

Crystal healing helps: Integration, coherence, a sense of belonging, spiritual ease

Crystals include:
- Amethyst
- Sugilite
- Clear quartz
- Charoite
- Tanzanite

Tantric painting illustrating the position of the chakras on the body of a meditating figure.

Amethyst

BROW

Position: Center of the forehead

Color: Indigo

Malfunctions: Depression, mental turmoil, anguish

Crystal healing helps:
Comprehension, perception, sense of perspective, vision, intuition, elevated awareness from the mundane world

Crystals include:
- Iolite
- Azurite
- Lapis lazuli
- Kyanite

Azurite

THROAT

Position: Base of the throat

Colors: Light blue, turquoise

Malfunctions: Stiff necks, sore throat, thyroid problems, hearing problems

Crystal healing helps:
Communication, expression, peace, understanding, heartfelt communication

Crystals include:
- Blue lace agate
- Celestite

Celestite

HEART

Position: Center of the chest

Colors: Green is associated with the upper heart chakra (unconditional love), while pink resonates powerfully with the lower heart chakra (human love)

Malfunctions: Lack of self-confidence, self-destructive tendencies, fear

Crystal healing helps: Relationships, empathy, harmony, balance, love

Crystals include:
• Emerald
• Malachite
• Moldavite
• Rhodonite
• Rose quartz
• Morganite

SOLAR PLEXUS

Position: Between the navel and the diaphragm

Color: Yellow

Malfunctions: Poor decision-making, low vitality, nervous and immune system problems

Crystal healing helps: Personal power, assuredness, self-reliance, digestion, joyfulness, integrity, self-confidence

Crystals include:
• Citrine
• Yellow topaz
• Pyrite
• Tiger's eye

Emerald

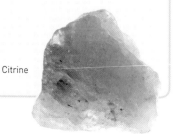

Citrine

SACRAL

Position: Just below the navel

Color: Orange

Malfunctions: Boredom, over-seriousness, disdain, holding on to the past, resentment, bladder and uterine disorders

Crystal healing helps: Creativity, exploration, enjoyment, pleasure, dynamism, curiosity, sensuality

Crystals include:
• Carnelian
• Copper
• Red jasper
• Amber

Carnelian

ROOT

Position: Base of the spine

Color: Red

Malfunctions: Obesity, hemorrhoids, constipation, problems associated with the feet, legs, bones, and blood, lethargy, insecurity, survival issues

Crystal healing helps: Physical energy levels, fitness, groundedness, practicality

Crystals include:
• Garnet
• Ruby
• Smoky quartz
• Black tourmaline
• Obsidian

Garnet

CHOOSING A PERSONAL STONE

THERE ARE NUMEROUS OF WAYS OF CHOOSING A CRYSTAL. YOU CAN SIMPLY CHOOSE ONE JUST BECAUSE YOU LIKE THE LOOK OF IT.

THE ROLE OF ATTRACTION

There is always a reason why one stone is noticed among many; why one almost indistinguishable tumbled stone feels more comfortable than another. It is a vital lesson to learn in order to gain an understanding and appreciation of our intuitive choices. Pay special attention to those stones that are very attractive to you because they will probably be the ones that are in harmony with your current state of subtle energy balance.

•

Likewise, notice the ones you instinctively dislike, since these will frequently represent qualities of subtle energy with which you cannot cope at the moment, but may subsequently feel drawn to when your body requires that energy for balance.

Listen to your intuition and allow it to attract you to the right stone.

You may experience physical sensations when holding the right stone in your hands.

ATTUNEMENT

When you are in harmony (attunement) with a crystal, you will often experience sensations of resonance. This could be that the crystal gives you feelings of wholeness and completion.

•

If you decide to hold a crystal or gemstone in your hand, you could get sensations such as heat or cold, tingling, or an electric-like charge; some people even feel pulsing sensations. These are all normal. In fact, the sensations can vary from person to person and from crystal to crystal.

•

There are no set rules; just allow your intuition to guide you. The more you set your intention to become a partner on this journey into the magical realms of the sacred stones, the more you allow wholeness, healing, and balance to manifest in your life.

Jewelry made from a particular stone, such as this string of carnelian beads, may hold a special appeal to you.

PLANETARY INFLUENCES

The link between heavenly bodies and gemstones has existed in India for at least 3,000 years. Ayurveda (Sanskrit, "life knowledge") is one of the world's oldest systems of medicine. Ayurveda gives a special role to gems through Vedic astrology. Jyotisha is the traditional Hindu system of astrology, also known as Hindu astrology, where the focus is on the ascendant planet at the time of birth. If you know your ascendant planet, you may be drawn to its related gemstone.

Moonstone

PLANETS AND GEMSTONES

Sun: Garnet, rubellite, ruby

Moon: Moonstone, pearl

Mercury: Emerald, green tourmaline, jade, malachite

Venus: Clear quartz, diamond

Mars: Carnelian, coral

Jupiter: Citrine, yellow topaz, yellow sapphire

Saturn: Blue sapphire, lapis lazuli, amethyst

Rahu (north lunar node): Hessonite, zircon

Ketu (south lunar node): Tiger's eye, cat's eye chrysoberyl

In Vedic astrology, there were nine stones related to the planets and the nodes of the Moon (points in space related to the movement of the Moon and the apparent movement of the Sun).

BIRTHSTONES

The link between heavenly bodies and gemstones is continued in the concept of birthstones in the western system of astrology. Birthstone lists vary greatly because some are arranged according to the zodiac (below) and some by calendar months (these are listed for each stone in the Crystal Directory). Many people are drawn to wearing their birthstone, and believe this to be an excellent way of exploring the properties of sacred crystals.

WESTERN ZODIAC BIRTHSTONES

Aries	Mar 21–Apr 19	Diamond
Taurus	Apr 20–May 20	Emerald
Gemini	May 21-Jun 20	Pearl
Cancer	Jun 21–Jul 22	Ruby
Leo	Jul 23–Aug 22	Peridot
Virgo	Aug 23–Sep 22	Blue sapphire
Libra	Sep 23-Oct 22	Opal
Scorpio	Oct 23–Nov 21	Topaz
Sagittarius	Nov 22–Dec 21	Turquoise, tanzanite
Capricorn	Dec 22–Jan 19	Garnet
Aquarius	Jan 20–Feb 18	Amethyst
Pisces	Feb 19–Mar 20	Aquamarine

Tanzanite

GETTING TO KNOW YOUR CRYSTAL

IN THIS SECTION WE EXPLORE SIMPLE WAYS OF
GETTING TO KNOW YOUR CRYSTAL.

GETTING STARTED

In order to increase your awareness and overall sensitivity, get
used to noticing the difference in how you feel before, during, and
after each session. The wisdom of crystals is sometimes very
subtle. Always find a quiet place to practice these techniques.

CLEANSING THE CRYSTAL

Before and after you use a crystal, it is a good idea to cleanse it in
some way because crystals have a tendency to absorb emotional
stress and other strong energy patterns. Simply holding your
crystal under running water is very effective. You just need to
first check that the crystal is not water-soluble.

CONTEMPLATION EXERCISE

It is hard to resist the allure of gazing at an attractive stone; this makes crystals an ideal focus for contemplation. This technique will help you to identify in which way the crystal is acting on your subtle energy systems, where we are often most sensitive to its characteristics.

1. Place the crystal on a flat surface a comfortable distance from you so that you can gaze on it in a relaxed way.

2. Sit quietly with your eyes closed for a moment.

3. Open your eyes and gaze at the crystal.

4. Close your eyes again and sit quietly.

5. Reach out and pick up your crystal and hold it with both hands, then close your eyes for a short while.

6. After several minutes, place the stone back in front of you.

7. Repeat this process, picking up the crystal and holding it with your eyes closed, and then placing it in front of you and gazing at it.

8. Notice any changes in how you feel.

9. It is a good idea to write down your experiences. This will increase your confidence and your ability to use your intuition.

A Buddhist master sitting in a meditation pose holding a dish filled with jewels. Clear or purple crystals are a good choice for raising the state of consciousness when meditating.

CRYSTAL MEDITATION

Many people use crystals to enhance and deepen their meditation practice. The meditation exercise opposite allows you to merge with the crystal consciousness. It is a good idea to learn how to ground yourself after these sessions. A simple technique is to imagine roots going out through of the soles of your feet into the center of the Earth.

Tibetan singing bowls are a type of bell, with the rim vibrating to produce a harmonic sound when rung. They are used as an aid to meditation along with crystals.

MEDITATION EXERCISE

1. Make yourself comfortable in a chair.

2. Hold your chosen crystal in your left hand.

3. Allow your eyes to close.

4. Begin to focus on your breath. Do not try to control your breathing, but simply be aware of the breath entering and leaving your body.

5. Gently begin to feel the crystal's subtle energy in your left hand. Feel the energy traveling up your left arm into your shoulder, then spreading across your chest and down your right arm, and flowing out of your fingers. Feel it gradually spreading through the whole of your physical body, flowing gently and easily until it slowly flows out of the top of your head and the soles of your feet.

6. At this point, begin to be aware of the space around your body as the crystal vibration flows all around you, totally enfolding you in a cloud of crystal energy. Feel yourself breathing this energy into your body until there is nothing but the gently oscillating crystal vibration. Now just relax even more and simply let go, floating on your own cloud of crystal energy.

7. When you are ready, allow your body to come back very slowly. Feel the weight of your body on the chair. Gradually become aware of your surroundings and your normal breathing pattern. Allow yourself a little time for any feelings of light-headedness to dissipate.

CRYSTAL
DIRECTORY

CLEAR QUARTZ

CLEAR QUARTZ INCREASES CLARITY OF THOUGHT, SHARPENS PERCEPTION, AND ENHANCES MEMORY.

CHAKRA PLACEMENT
Crown, all others

SPIRIT GUIDE
Archangel Metatron

BIRTHSTONE
April

APPEARANCE

Clear quartz is transparent.

HEALING

Clear quartz is the "master healer" or "cure all" of the crystal world. It amplifies and increases the harmony of the energies of all other stones when it is placed nearby.

•

It has a long history of being used for divination and scrying, bringing clarity of mind and revealing the truth. It quickly removes energetic blocks from all the chakras. It is used for amplifying your concentrated attention and intent when healing energy is directed through the clear quartz crystal.

•

It also allows easy access to altered states of consciousness, and will assist the movement of energy flowing between the chakras. A clear quartz crystal placed anywhere in the aura will help bring balance. It is often used for meditation practice and kundalini activation.

ABALONE

ABALONE BALANCES THE EMOTIONS, INCREASING OPEN-MINDEDNESS
AND FLEXIBILITY. IT HELPS US TO GO WITH THE FLOW.

CHAKRA PLACEMENT
Crown,
all others

SPIRIT GUIDE
Archangel
Muriel

BIRTHSTONE
July

APPEARANCE

Abalone shell has a range of iridescent pastel rainbow colors.

HEALING

Abalone and other types of shells have been used for decorative purposes by many cultures for millennia. Abalone that displays more than one color can be extremely useful for healing because it will introduce a blend of color energies simultaneously.

•

Abalone is used for healing the emotions to bring harmony. It is especially useful for handling and calming emotional situations. It teaches us to flow with these feelings to help us develop our sensitivity to others.

•

In crystal healing it is helpful for arthritis and other joint disorders, muscle problems, the heart, and digestion. Abalone shell is an excellent companion when needing guidance in relationships. It fosters feelings of cooperation because it aids communication and compromise.

PURPLE FLUORITE

PURPLE FLUORITE FACILITATES ASSIMILATION OF NEW IDEAS AND FINE LEVELS OF AWARENESS. IT ENCOURAGES INNOVATION AND INVENTION.

CHAKRA PLACEMENT
Crown

SPIRIT GUIDE
Archangel Zadkiel

BIRTHSTONE
January

APPEARANCE

Purple fluorite ranges in color from pale lilac to deep purple-black and from transparent to opaque.

HEALING

Purple fluorite is an excellent meditation stone. Meditating with this crystal will help release your immense potential; it helps clear your mind and improve concentration. This improves your health and can rejuvenate your body.

Fluorite restores the energy structure of your body and aura. This can awaken healing and personal growth, and even improve your creativity and innovation skills.

Fluorite helps you in the decision-making process because it brings structure to the mental body, which clears negative thought forms that may have lodged in your neural pathways. When you learn to control your mind, you can change your life and shift into a higher joyous vibration.

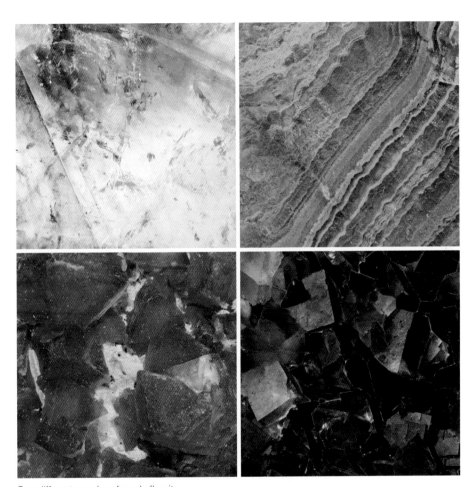

Four different samples of purple fluorite.

AMETHYST

AMETHYST HAS BEEN PRIZED FOR ITS BEAUTY AND
LEGENDARY ENERGIES FOR THOUSANDS OF YEARS.

CHAKRA PLACEMENT
Crown

SPIRIT GUIDE
Archangel
Zadkiel

BIRTHSTONE
February

APPEARANCE

Amethyst is a member of the quartz family. Its color varies
from pale to deep purple.

HEALING

Amethyst has a broad spectrum of healing energies, so it is
an effective healer of most conditions. It helps to neutralize
pain, so it can be placed over any painful area. It eases
headache and migraine.

Amethyst is emotionally soothing, so it is used to ease
stress and emotional exhaustion. Being a classic meditation
tool, amethyst aids meditation by calming and focusing an
overactive mind. It also eases addictions and addictive traits
within the personality, allowing the potential for change
and growth.

Amethyst is a stone of spiritual protection, bringing clear-
headed and quick thinking.

SUGILITE

SUGILITE IS A MAGICAL DREAM STONE THAT
GROUNDS MYSTICAL EXPERIENCES.

CHAKRA PLACEMENT
Crown

SPIRIT GUIDE
Archangel Zadkiel

BIRTHSTONE
December

APPEARANCE

Sugilite is opaque and comes in all shades of purple, often with black manganese inclusions.

HEALING

Sugilite is known as the stone of forgiveness through love. It teaches you to honor, respect, and nurture yourself. It gives protection from negative energies, and is highly nurturing to the emotional body. This means it has been utilized by very sensitive souls who find it difficult to screen out the hostility of others.

•

Sugilite helps us to achieve our spiritual goals by developing our psychic gifts. It can bring unprecedented growth and development. Many people on the spiritual path use sugilite for grounding their meditation experiences into their everyday life.

•

Sugilite brings peace, dignity, humanitarianism, and mental creativity. It has been used to clear headaches and migraine, as well as ease emotional problems related to stress.

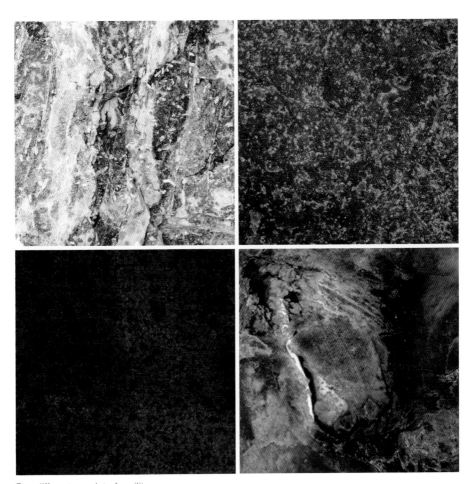

Four different samples of sugilite.

CHAROITE

CHAROITE BRINGS A CALM PERSPECTIVE TO HELP YOU
ADAPT TO TURBULENT NEW CIRCUMSTANCES.

**CHAKRA
PLACEMENT**
Crown,
heart

SPIRIT GUIDE
Archangel
Tzaphkiel

BIRTHSTONE
February

APPEARANCE

Charoite ranges in color from deep purple to pale lilac.
It has a rich internal patterning, interspaced with translucent
patches and inclusions of black aegirine.

HEALING

Charoite enhances intuition, meditation, and relaxation.
It expands the energy of the "higher mind."

•

It quickens and awakens our consciousness, allowing our
personal life plan to gently unfold. It guides us to follow that
path to reach our highest potential.

•

Charoite accelerates transformation and purification when
placed on the crown chakra. To bring peace and quieten and
soothe the central nervous system, place a charoite crystal
above the head and also at the base of the skull. To ease a
troubled heart and release unconscious fears, place charoite
on the heart chakra.

LEPIDOLITE WITH RUBELLITE

THIS IS ONE OF THE MOST EMOTIONALLY COMFORTING COMBINATIONS.

CHAKRA PLACEMENT
Crown, heart

SPIRIT GUIDE
Archangels Tzaphkiel and Chamuel

BIRTHSTONE
February

APPEARANCE

Lepidolite with rubellite is a pinkish, lilac gray with deep pink tourmaline crystals.

HEALING

This crystal is a powerful agent for calming and healing the emotional body and insulating the heart from hurtful energies. It is often used for dream work. When used for magical purposes, it gives protection by confusing enemies.

•

Physically, lepidolite works on the glands and immune system. It can also desensitize the nervous system, which decreases stress, anxiety, and depression. Emotionally it is transformational, enhancing love, patience, and optimism. Mentally, lepidolite stimulates the intellect, giving encouragement. It fosters calmness, trust, and acceptance.

•

Spiritually, it aids meditation practice by cleansing the aura of emotional stress, allowing quiet, soothing, deep contemplation to flow. Lepidolite helps the grieving process and is supportive in times of change or trauma.

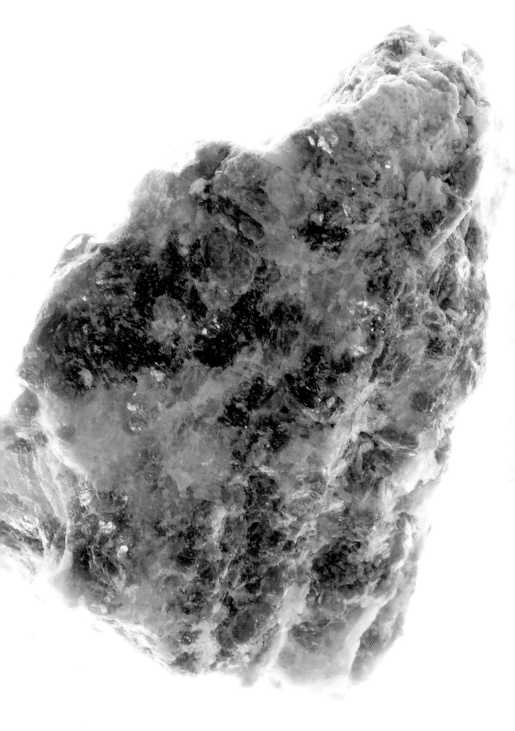

IOLITE

IOLITE INCREASES THE POTENTIAL FOR CHANGE AND THE GROWTH OF
SPIRITUAL AWARENESS. IT AWAKENS OUR INHERENT TALENTS.

CHAKRA PLACEMENT
Brow

SPIRIT GUIDE
Archangel
Raziel

BIRTHSTONE
December

APPEARANCE

Iolite, also known as water sapphire, is a transparent to
translucent shade of blue-violet.

HEALING

Iolite awakens psychic abilities and enhances our intuition.
It works on the brow chakra, bringing clairvoyance and
insight, which in turn brings confidence in our own instinctive
abilities. Intuition is the sum of information that is received
by the mind at levels of awareness that we do not
usually access.

●

Iolite supports the healing of the eyes and sinuses. It calms
the nervous and endocrine systems as well as easing
headaches. It is used to counteract insomnia, nightmares,
and night terrors. It can also ease addictions and addictive
traits within the personality.

●

Iolite is a visionary stone of protection.

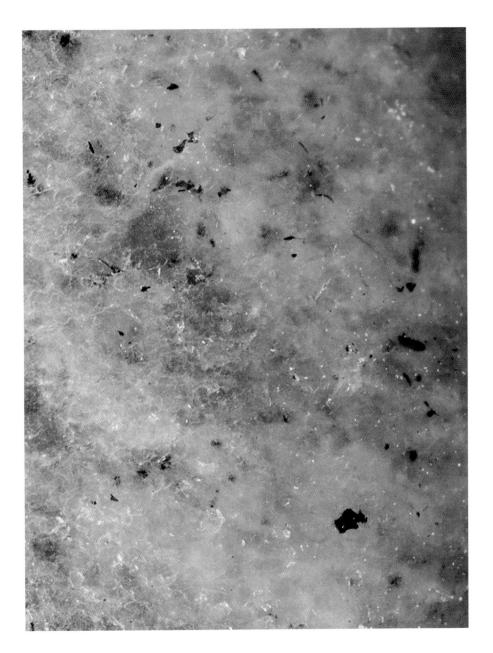

TANZANITE

TANZANITE BRINGS RADICAL SHIFTS IN CONSCIOUSNESS. IT ENLIVENS CONTACT
AND COMMUNICATION WITH OTHER REALMS AND DIMENSIONS.

CHAKRA PLACEMENT
Brow

SPIRIT GUIDE
Archangel
Tzaphkiel

BIRTHSTONE
December

APPEARANCE

Tanzanite is as rare as it is beautiful. It is transparent to translucent shades of deep blue-violet, lilac, or pale bluish.

HEALING

Tanzanite aligns the heart and mind to bring peace and tranquillity. It is soothing to all the body systems. It calmly stimulates psychic abilities.

•

Tanzanite awakens us to altered states of reality and our perception from the mundane to the magical. It is a stone of sacred contemplation that is used for meditation.

•

Physically it eases headaches, migraine, and insomnia. Emotionally it eases worries and allows us to feel more compassionate, loving, and heart center focused. It calms an overactive mind, bringing peaceful relief from anxiety, fear, and self-doubt. Tanzanite turns us on to the importance of developing our spiritual life.

KYANITE

KYANITE ENHANCES PSYCHIC, CLAIRVOYANT, AND TELEPATHIC ABILITIES BY STIMULATING THE BROW CHAKRA.

CHAKRA PLACEMENT
Brow

SPIRIT GUIDE
Archangel Michael

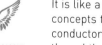

BIRTHSTONE
August

APPEARANCE

Kyanite forms in blade-like, opaque blue crystals. Gem quality can be transparent.

HEALING

Kyanite has a swift, focused action. It transfers energy very quickly. It is used to remove blockages, cutting away wrong mental, emotional, and spiritual attitudes that may hold you captive, enslaved in a victim mentality.

•

It is like a double-edged sword, so you can cut away dualistic concepts that have blinded you to the truth. It is an excellent conductor of life energy and is used to build bridges between the subtle energy systems of the physical, emotional, mental, and spiritual bodies.

•

Kyanite reduces fevers and high blood pressure, calming hot conditions where there is too much heat in the body. It eases stiff necks and stiff neck attitudes, and heals ear and throat infections.

AZURITE

AZURITE IS A STONE OF MYSTERY AND MAGIC. IT ENHANCES ALL
CLAIRVOYANT ABILITIES, BRINGING INSIGHT AND CLARITY.

CHAKRA PLACEMENT
Brow, throat

SPIRIT GUIDE
Archangel Raziel

BIRTHSTONE
December

APPEARANCE

Azurite ranges in color from azure to deep blue or pale blue.
It is opaque.

HEALING

Azurite swiftly dissolves fear into comprehension. It draws
out memories or old stress, allowing them to be released in
healing. Often our fears and phobias are deeply rooted within
the subconscious level, often placed there during our
formative years.

•

Azurite is very useful for healing all stress-related disorders.
It is an excellent meditation stone because it brings ease to
the spiritual body and strengthens the astral body.

•

Azurite can help with a wide range of problems, including
a dysfunctional throat chakra, such as sore throats, stiff
necks, and thyroid problems; hearing problems, tinnitus, and
asthma; emotional problems such as being over-talkative,
dogmatic, self-righteous, or arrogant; holding back from
self-expression; and unreliability and inconsistency of views.

LAPIS LAZULI

THIS HEAVENLY BLUE STONE IS ASSOCIATED WITH TRUTH, BALANCE, AND JUSTICE. IT ENCOURAGES DETERMINATION AND FORTITUDE.

CHAKRA PLACEMENT
Brow, throat

SPIRIT GUIDE
Archangel Michael

BIRTHSTONE
September

APPEARANCE

Lapis is deep blue with white calcite streaks and gold flecks of pyrite.

HEALING

Lapis lazuli is a high-intensity etheric blue stone. It contains the energies of royalty, wisdom, patience, honesty, mental attainment, truthful communication, contentment, artistic inspiration, deep meditation, spiritual and philosophical contemplation, personal integrity, and loyalty.

•

It is the "spirit of truth." It activates the brow and throat chakras, and is used for deep meditation and journeying to seek the spiritual guidance of the ancestors. Lapis lazuli is a stone of high initiation that is particularly attractive to those with a past-life connection to Egypt.

•

It works well with the throat, jaw, and upper chest areas. It is an effective cleanser, drawing tension and anxiety to the surface.

48

LABRADORITE

LABRADORITE IS A STONE OF MAGICAL ENCHANTMENT. IT IS
A TRULY FASCINATINGLY, BEAUTIFUL, COLORFUL MINERAL.

CHAKRA PLACEMENT
Brow,
throat

SPIRIT GUIDE
Archangel
Raziel

BIRTHSTONE
November

APPEARANCE

Labradorite is noted for its stunning iridescence; this unique
effect is known as "labradorescence." It has a remarkable
play of color that shows vivid flashes of violet, blue, green,
gold, and orange.

HEALING

In metaphysical circles labradorite is known as the "bringer
of light." It illuminates our spiritual path to personal
enlightenment. It works by dispelling darkness.

•

Labradorite enhances our ability to focus on personal issues
without letting outside influences affect us. It is a protective,
shielding stone that creates a force field of auric defense.

•

Labradorite can aid in uncovering unconscious and
subconscious belief patterns that can cause unpleasant
emotional states. Labradorite heals relationships—it shows
you where there is no substance, just delusion and denial.

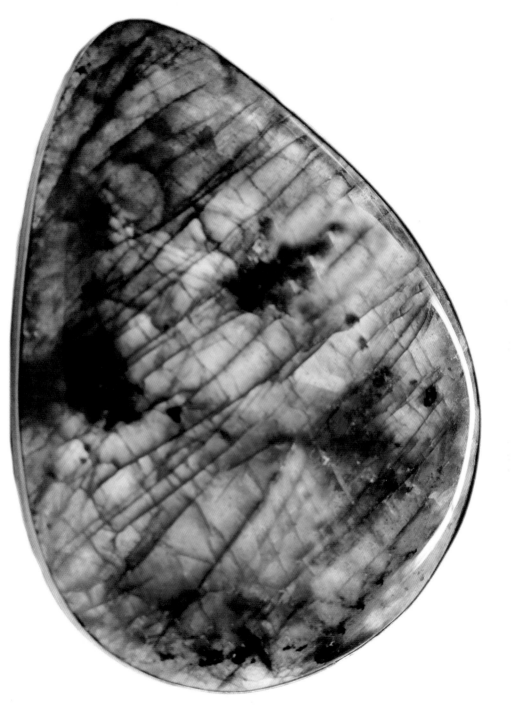

PEACOCK ORE

PEACOCK ORE ENHANCES CREATIVE EXPRESSION
BY INCREASING INNOVATION.

CHAKRA PLACEMENT
Brow, throat, solar plexus

SPIRIT GUIDE
Archangel Yehadriel

BIRTHSTONE
August

APPEARANCE

Peacock ore has a metallic, brassy array of violets, purples, blues, reds, pinks, and yellows.

HEALING

Peacock ore encourages optimism and silences unwanted, undesirable thoughts. It removes energetic emotional blocks. Metaphysically it represents the union of beauty and power, a balance of the male and female polarities.

•

It is magical, bringing unexpected sudden change and serendipity. It allows us to be flexible in our thought processes and stops us from getting into a rut, allowing a free-flowing emotional experience.

•

It stimulates the nervous system and is used to supplement the life force, which can stop mental fog. It can be used to ground and protect our energies, which keeps us from feeling "spaced out" after mental exertion. It helps us to accomplish challenging tasks with ease.

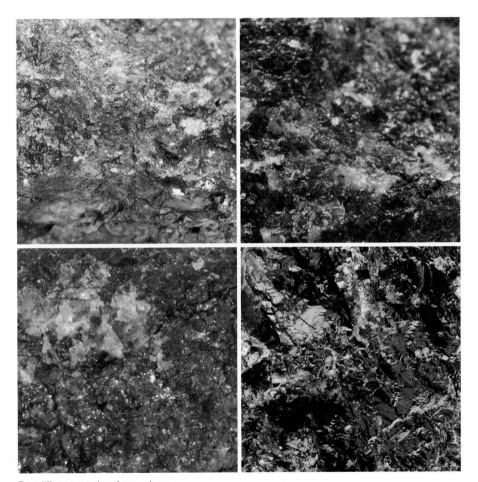

Four different samples of peacock ore.

MOONSTONE

MOONSTONE IS A STONE OF SWEET MYSTERY, SELF-DISCOVERY,
INSIGHT, INTUITION, IMAGININGS, AND DREAMS.

CHAKRA PLACEMENT
Brow, heart, sacral

SPIRIT GUIDE
Archangel Auriel

BIRTHSTONE
June

APPEARANCE

Moonstone has a soft blue-white pearly luster that can vary depending on structure. It can show opalescence or rainbow iridescence and schiller (a metallic luster).

HEALING

Moonstone is the stone of the high priestess, the divine feminine aspect of creation. Its soft hues remind us of the moon's reflective light.

•

Moonstone attunes us to the cycles of time; it is associated with fertility, flow, and progression. It is a potent aid to developing intuition and emotional understanding. It is nurturing to the soul, and heals the subtle energy systems by comforting and supporting serene contemplation.

•

It aids peaceful sleep, relieves indigestion, and balances the body's lymphatic system. It also relieves menstrual cramps and eases other female issues, especially water retention.

BLUE LACE AGATE

BLUE LACE AGATE IS STRENGTHENING, AIDING COMMUNICATION, SELF-EXPRESSION, CONFIDENCE, COMFORT, AND CLARITY.

CHAKRA PLACEMENT
Throat

SPIRIT GUIDE
Archangel Arkiel

BIRTHSTONE
March

APPEARANCE

Blue lace agate has distinct intricate bands of soft violet-blue, white, and gray.

HEALING

This cooling, calming stone can be used anywhere there is a build-up of energy. It definitely brings ease and will aid overall well-being.

•

Blue lace agate eases stiff necks and stiff neck attitudes, and heals ear and throat infections. It is very beneficial for children or those who have difficulty making themselves heard or understood by others; it assists in becoming more articulate in your speech. It helps you find the right words to express yourself.

•

It brings clarity of thought and will balance and strengthen the throat chakra. Because all agates are slow to act but incredibly stable, it is best to wear it as a pendant for long periods of time.

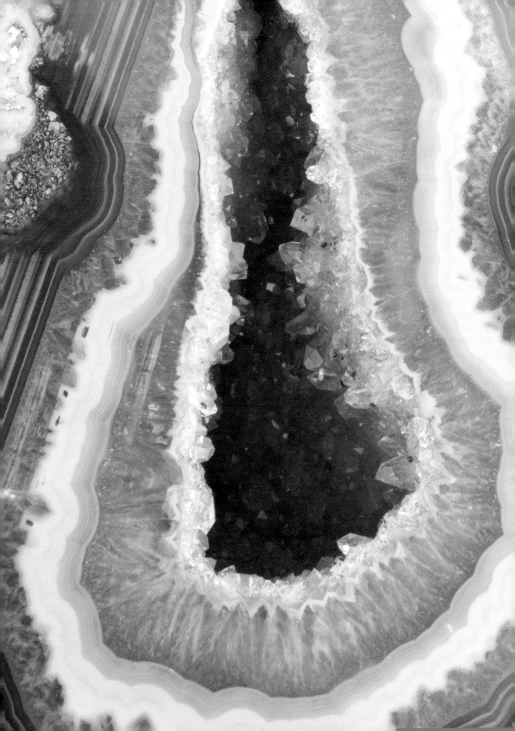

CELESTITE

HEAVENLY CELESTITE IS USED TO CONTACT YOUR GUARDIAN ANGEL
AND DEVELOP PSYCHIC ABILITIES.

CHAKRA PLACEMENT
Throat

SPIRIT GUIDE
Guardian angels

BIRTHSTONE
February

APPEARANCE

Celestite, also known as celestine, is sky blue and transparent to opaque.

HEALING

Celestite offers gentle, uplifting angelic communication and expanded awareness of the higher dimensions. It brings inner peace, spiritual expansion, tranquillity, calm, soul harmony, and focus to the highest realm of heavenly light.

•

Celestite links strongly with your guardian angels. Those who choose to work with this high vibration feel they are blessed with a sunny, harmonious, joyful disposition. Celestite enhances clairvoyance and visionary skills. It is calming to the emotional body; it is especially useful as a shield for people who suffer inner conflict because they absorb other people's emotional stress and discord.

•

Physically celestite lowers blood pressure and eases stomach problems and nervous stress. Celestite is inspiring; it opens the mind to new ideas.

SODALITE

SODALITE QUIETENS AN OVERACTIVE MIND AND IS STABILIZING
TO THE EMOTIONS. IT ENCOURAGES CALMNESS.

**CHAKRA
PLACEMENT**
Throat

SPIRIT GUIDE
Archangel
Cassiel

BIRTHSTONE
December

APPEARANCE

Sodalite is an opaque, rich royal blue stone with veins of
white calcite.

HEALING

Sodalite enhances mental performance because it is calming
to the nervous system; it eases pressure and worries. It is
almost hypnotically boring (soporific) and slows everything
down, so it is good to ease chronic insomnia.

•

Sodalite can aid the development of latent psychic abilities,
especially for those people who are just beginning to develop
these gifts.

•

It is useful in the treatment of sore throats. It is calming to
the emotions and can ease panic attacks. It is useful if you
have to speak in public, especially if this sometimes makes
you fearful. It aids restful sleep in children. It is used to
regulate blood pressure and ease water retention. It
cleanses the lymphatic system, which will enhance the
immune system.

AQUAMARINE

AQUAMARINE WAS BELIEVED TO BE THE TREASURE OF THE MERMAIDS,
AND WAS USED AS A TALISMAN TO BRING GOOD FORTUNE.

**CHAKRA
PLACEMENT**
Throat

SPIRIT GUIDE
Archangel
Muriel

BIRTHSTONE
March

APPEARANCE

Aquamarine is the blue-green variety of beryl. Its name
derives from Latin, meaning "water of the sea."

HEALING

The serene color of aquamarine is said to cool the temper,
allowing the wearer to remain calm and level-headed in all
situations. It does this by clarifying perception.

•

Aquamarine boosts the immune system and balances
the throat chakra by clearing stagnant emotions. This
encourages optimism, enabling creative expression and
ideas to flow freely.

•

Aquamarine eases problems with the ears, nose, throat, and
nervous system. It also eases panic attacks, seasickness,
and phobias. Possibly the most important quality of
aquamarine is that it gives freedom from the impressions
and influences of others.

BLUE SAPPHIRE

BLUE SAPPHIRE IS A HEAVENLY BLUE STONE THAT
ENCOURAGES YOU TO REACH FOR THE STARS.

CHAKRA PLACEMENT
Throat

SPIRIT GUIDE
Archangel
Cassiel

BIRTHSTONE
September

APPEARANCE

Blue sapphire is transparent and comes in all shades of
blue. Low grade is opaque.

HEALING

Blue sapphire gives inspirational support, encouraging
you to reach for high spiritual attainment. It can release you
from emotional bondage. Wearing or carrying this gorgeous
gemstone encourages you to become a seeker of truth.

It works primarily on the throat chakra, and also on the
endocrine system and thyroid and parathyroid glands. Its
energy vibration also covers the upper lungs, shoulders,
and base of the skull.

It counteracts the psychological problems of speaking
in public. Blue sapphire also instills patience and peace.
It helps you to reason things out slowly and quietly with
integrity. It also teaches discretion, moderation, wisdom,
and discernment. It is an excellent meditation crystal to
use when you find it difficult to clear your mind.

TURQUOISE

TURQUOISE IS A POPULAR PROTECTIVE AMULET. IT IS POSSIBLY
THE LONGEST USED TALISMAN OF ALL STONES.

CHAKRA PLACEMENT
Throat, heart

SPIRIT GUIDE
Archangel Sarahiel

BIRTHSTONE
April

APPEARANCE

Turquoise is an opaque light blue to blue-green stone.

HEALING

Turquoise is a healer of the emotions of the heart. It teaches you to speak from the heart. It loves the sharing of emotional wisdom, wholeness, and truthful, heartfelt communication; it loves togetherness and family. It brings people together and gets them communicating.

•

Turquoise is a good crystal to carry if you have to speak in public. It calms the nerves and "feeds" the central nervous system, so it is helpful in healing nervous stress or breakdown, as well easing panic attacks or emotional shock.

•

Turquoise balances all the subtle energy systems, especially the throat and heart chakras. It also eases asthma and bronchitis. Turquoise makes an excellent meditation stone because it enhances and strengths the aura.

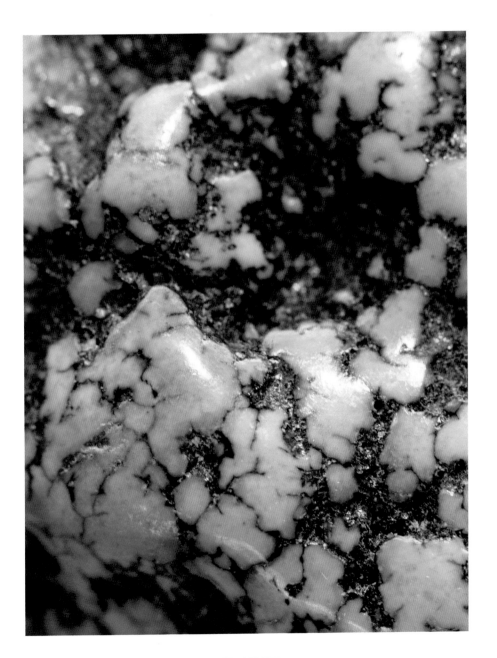

CHRYSOCOLLA

CHRYSOCOLLA EMANATES THE GENTLENESS AND POWER OF THE SACRED
FEMININE ENERGY. IT IS A GODDESS STONE THAT SPEAKS TO THE SOUL.

CHAKRA PLACEMENT
Throat, heart

SPIRIT GUIDE
Archangel Shamael

BIRTHSTONE
May

APPEARANCE
Most commonly the color is blue, green, or blue-green.

HEALING
Chrysocolla has a strong affinity and is closely attuned to the resonance of the earth. It is a stone of communication, unity, harmony, and benevolence.

•

Chrysocolla stimulates the throat chakra to aid clear, heartfelt communication. It is used in magic to bring success and peace. It is closely associated with "sacred sound" and will amplify the potency of mantras, invocations, and prayer.

•

Physically it is used to relax breathing and increase expressive ability. It assists in the gentle release of stress, anxiety, trauma, and other fear-based imbalances that cause digestive and emotional upset.

AMAZONITE

AN AMAZONITE SCARAB RING WAS AMONG THE TREASURES FOUND IN TUTANKHAMEN'S TOMB. IT IS THE STONE OF HARMONY AND PROTECTION.

CHAKRA PLACEMENT
Throat, heart, solar plexus

SPIRIT GUIDE
Archangel Barachiel

BIRTHSTONE
August

APPEARANCE

The depth of amazonite's green or blue-green color varies considerably. It is opaque.

HEALING

Amazonite is often the recommended treatment for osteoporosis and tooth decay. It aids calcium absorption and eases muscle spasms and sprains. Its blue to green color is soothing to the nervous system and aligns the etheric body with the physical body.

•

It has a beneficial influence on the throat and heart chakras, and is often used to balance the thymus gland that lies midway between the two chakra points. Amazonite eases problems with the throat, ears, nose, carpal tunnel system, and nervous system.

•

It helps strengthen self-identity and personal power when placed on the solar plexus chakra. It has also been used in past-life work and to contact the ancestors.

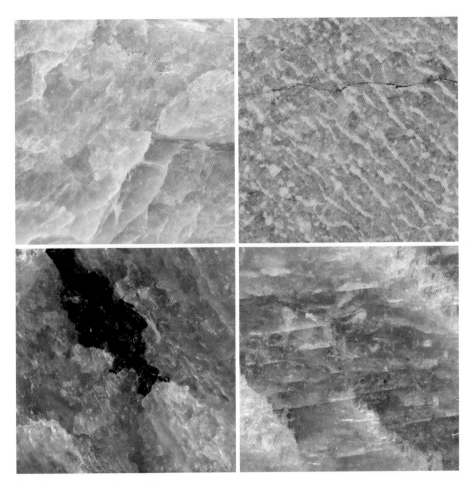

Four different samples of amazonite.

KUNZITE

KUNZITE OPENS THE HEART TO SPIRITUAL LOVE,
THE DIVINE LOVE THAT UNDERPINS ALL OF CREATION.

CHAKRA PLACEMENT
Heart (upper)

SPIRIT GUIDE
Shekinah
(the Eternal
Shekinah El)

BIRTHSTONE
March

APPEARANCE

Kunzite can be opaque or transparent to translucent. Its color ranges from pale pink to deep pinky lilac.

HEALING

Love, support, understanding, enhanced self-esteem, protection, counteraction to aggression, harmony—these are all the wonderful gifts that kunzite energy bestows on those who choose to use it for crystal healing.

•

Kunzite has a great balance of compassion, peace, and freedom. Kunzite does have a hidden magic—it can reveal and heal a lost childhood where, due to circumstances, you had to grow up too soon.

•

It is used to support healing of the emotions, as it eases nervous stress and supports the para-sympathetic nervous system. It also provides invaluable protection during difficult emotional times. Ideally you would wear it as a pendant.

RHODOCHROSITE

RHODOCHROSITE IS A STONE OF EMOTIONAL WELL-BEING. IT BRINGS
THE ENERGY OF CREATIVE SELF-EXPRESSION AND COMPASSION.

CHAKRA PLACEMENT
Heart (upper)

SPIRIT GUIDE
Archangel
Raguel

BIRTHSTONE
August

APPEARANCE

In massive form it has concentric bands of pink, rose,
peachy pink, and white, which appear when it is cut and
polished. Large, transparent, single-colored crystals are
an intense rose red.

HEALING

Rhodochrosite is not the delicate, loving energy of the rose
quartz pink, but rather the active energy of spiritual love in
action, which is compassion. Rhodochrosite brings ease
within the self and allows us to appreciate our own unique
talents and abilities.

•

It eases difficulties within the digestive and reproductive
systems. It also assists in clearing pain, anger, and anxiety
by relieving tension and stress.

•

When placed on the heart center, it helps us to develop
compassion and understanding. Rhodochrosite is excellent
for those who need to heal their "inner child."

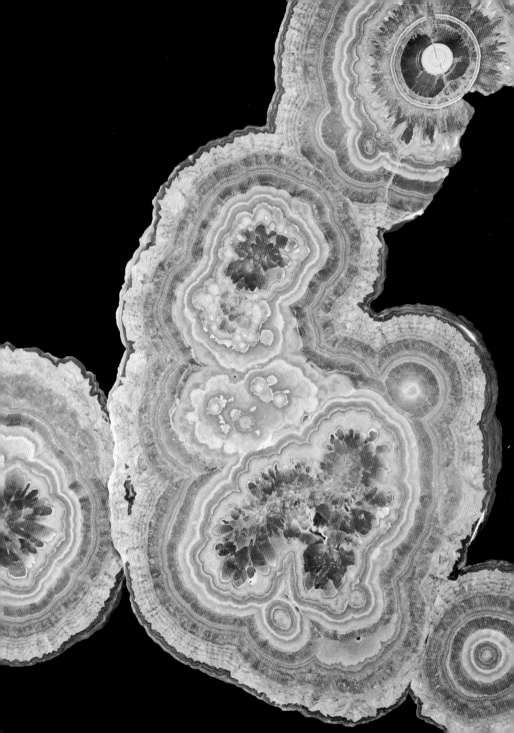

ROSE QUARTZ

ROSE QUARTZ IS ONE OF THE MOST PLEASANTLY SEDUCTIVE
VARIETIES OF QUARTZ. IT IS THE ULTIMATE STONE OF LOVE.

**CHAKRA
PLACEMENT**
Heart (upper)

SPIRIT GUIDE
Archangel
Chamuel

BIRTHSTONE
May

APPEARANCE

Rose quartz is renowned for its delicate pink tones.
It is usually found in its translucent massive form,
only occasionally growing in clusters of small crystals.

HEALING

Rose quartz transmits a soft, loving energy that is soothing
and calming to the emotions and can fully balance the
emotional body.

•

The rose quartz ray of healing works dynamically on
the heart center. It gently cleanses and transmutes all
stored negative issues of self-worth, self-confidence,
and self-acceptance.

•

It contains within its beautiful pink mandala the ray of hope.
It is ideal to carry or wear in stressful situations to prevent
the build-up of anxiety. It is good to place this crystal on the
heart chakra after trauma, injury, or surgery.

Four different samples of rose quartz.

MORGANITE

MORGANITE RADIATES THE ENERGY OF LOVE, PEACE, AND COMPASSION.
IT MELTS BOUNDARIES TO MAKE EVERYTHING SEEM POSSIBLE.

CHAKRA PLACEMENT
Heart (upper)

SPIRIT GUIDE
Isda (angel of nourishment)

BIRTHSTONE
February

APPEARANCE

Morganite is the transparent to translucent pink to peachy pink variety of beryl.

HEALING

Morganite emanates the energy of compassion; the love of humanity, of honoring each being for his or her own unique expression of their intrinsic divinity; of unity within diversity.

•

Morganite's energy signature or resonance is very special. It holds the emotional body stable as you let go of pain and painful memories; this is the key to its use. It gives you the courage to move forward with your life and not be a victim of your past. It teaches you to take a deep breath and relax.

•

Physically morganite works on the digestive system; affection is nourishment. It heals parts of the body and emotions that we have judged unlovely or unlovable.

RHODONITE

RHODONITE ASSISTS YOU IN DEVELOPING MATURE EMOTIONAL
STRENGTH AND UNIVERSAL LOVE AND COMPASSION.

CHAKRA PLACEMENT
Heart (upper)

SPIRIT GUIDE
Archangel
Chamuel

BIRTHSTONE
May

APPEARANCE

Rhodonite is an opaque rose pink with black inclusions of manganese oxide.

HEALING

Rhodonite helps you discover and develop your lost or hidden talents. These are the talents you may have displayed in childhood but suppressed due to the limitations of your surroundings or upbringing.

•

It is especially supportive through times of uncertainty or transformation, particularly if the change was not of your choosing. Rhodonite helps to dispel negative states of mind, confusion, and anxiety. It works primarily on the heart chakra but it can be safely used on the sacral chakra or throat to unblock communication channels.

•

It eases co-dependency and feelings of melancholia or fears concerning loneliness, commitment, or betrayal by making your deep needs manifest themselves. It is used for dream work, allowing clarity and understanding of subtle messages.

RUBELLITE

RUBELLITE IS THE HIGHLY PRIZED RED FORM OF TOURMALINE
AND HAS A DEEP RESONANCE WITH THE HEART CHAKRA.

CHAKRA PLACEMENT
Heart (upper), root

SPIRIT GUIDE
Archangel Chamuel

BIRTHSTONE
July

APPEARANCE

Rubellite's name is derived from the similarity of its color to that of ruby, although most rubellite is considerably more pink than red.

HEALING

Rubellite is a powerful heart chakra stone that strengthens your wisdom, empathy, compassion, and willpower. Your creativity is enhanced as you open yourself to the everyday beauty that surrounds you.

•

Rubellite melts the boundaries you may have erected between yourself and others. It makes everything seem possible; it makes you feel receptive and relaxed.

•

It aids those who may have become passive in rediscovering their zest for living, assisting in finding the inner courage and strength to face and change the situation. In crystal therapy rubellite directly links the heart and root chakras to bring balance.

WATERMELON TOURMALINE

THIS STONE BRINGS BALANCE, HARMONY, AND JOY TO THE HEART.

CHAKRA PLACEMENT
Heart (upper)

SPIRIT GUIDE
Archangels Chamuel and Raphael

BIRTHSTONE
May

APPEARANCE

Watermelon tourmaline is transparent. The color is always pink interior and green exterior.

HEALING

Watermelon tourmaline is one of the foremost healing crystals; its unique properties make it second to none in this respect.

It holds the best combination of colors to balance the heart chakra. It assists in releasing old emotional pain and trauma with love. It is used to treat all stress and nervous conditions.

It is especially helpful during stormy periods in relationships. It will cool, balance, and calm the emotions, so is also good when you are trying to make up your mind; it will bring you back to the center of yourself. It will also melt any fears you have of committing to the healing process.

JADE

JADE IS A STONE OF PEACE AND TRANQUILLITY. IT REPRESENTS HEAVENLY
HARMONY AND HAPPINESS IN BUSINESS AND FAMILY RELATIONSHIPS.

**CHAKRA
PLACEMENT**
Heart (lower)

SPIRIT GUIDE
Archangel
Raphael

BIRTHSTONE
July

APPEARANCE

Jade comes in many colors, including green, blue, black, red,
purple, and white. It is always opaque.

HEALING

Green jade brings peacefulness; it instills wisdom and
promotes feelings of effortless ease. It cleanses feelings
of self-disgust and self-loathing, bringing stability to
the personality.

•

This stone harmonizes relationships on all levels and heals
nervous stress caused by outside influences. Green jade is
conventionally a stone of abundance, and it is used to
manifest wealth and security.

•

It is often used to ease kidney problems. It is also associated
with longevity and connecting with your ancestors and the
spirits of the dead. On an emotional level it balances the
heart chakra, which helps improve relationships.

GREEN FLUORITE

GREEN FLUORITE BRINGS LIFE-SUPPORTING CALM, ALLOWING
US TO RELATE POSITIVELY WITH THE WORLD AROUND US.

CHAKRA PLACEMENT
Heart (lower)

SPIRIT GUIDE
Archangel
Raphael

BIRTHSTONE
June

APPEARANCE

This comes in all shades of transparent to translucent green.

HEALING

Green fluorite harmonizes the heart chakra, bringing emotional stability. It can release subconscious hidden knowledge and intuitive forces.

•

We are a magnetic field of energy; we attract exactly what we need. What we dwell on day after day is recorded in our auric field—the database of the mind. Green fluorite teaches you, through one-pointed concentration, to manifest positive energy into your life; it also helps you to clear out the negative thoughts.

•

It is an auric cleanser; as such it will release destructive thought forms and chronic conditions that have lodged there. When you learn to harness the power of your mind, you can change your life, keying into a higher vibration of the higher emotions and higher consciousness.

HIDDENITE

HIDDENITE BRINGS THE GENTLE GREEN RAY OF TENDER HEART HEALING,

OF HOPE AND FRAGILE NEW BEGINNINGS.

CHAKRA PLACEMENT
Heart (lower)

SPIRIT GUIDE
Archangel
Ambriel

BIRTHSTONE
May

APPEARANCE

The color range of hiddenite is yellow-green or emerald green. It can be transparent to opaque.

HEALING

Hiddenite releases feelings of failure; it is good for those who put on a brave face when their heart is full of pain. It helps them to honor these feelings by acknowledging them and then gently release them.

•

Hiddenite works on the heart, thymus, shoulders, chest, and lungs. We store deep sorrow in our lungs and this can cause recurring chest infections due to a weakened immune system.

•

When combined with its sister crystal kunzite (they are both from the spodumene family of crystals), it can stabilize the emotional body to give comfort, supporting us to rediscover the blissful joy of interpersonal relationships.

MALACHITE

MALACHITE BRINGS BALANCE AND HARMONY TO THE HEART. IT HAS
LONG BEEN ASSOCIATED WITH PERSONAL GROWTH AND ABUNDANCE.

**CHAKRA
PLACEMENT**
Heart (lower)

SPIRIT GUIDE
Archangel
Suriel

BIRTHSTONE
May

APPEARANCE

The banding of different shades of green and its concentric
eye patterns easily distinguish malachite from other
green minerals.

HEALING

Malachite is an ideal stone for clearing emotional confusion,
which is often caused by stress. Healing requires creating a
peaceful space to allow receptivity to the energy of change.

•

Malachite helps to create the fine balance that we need
in order to live harmoniously with the world without
suppressing it.

•

Malachite can assist in restoring vitality and strength after
illness, surgery, or exhaustion. It is used to release toxins
from the body and alleviate rheumatism. It is an effective
pain reliever when placed over the painful body area.
Malachite instills confidence and personal responsibility.

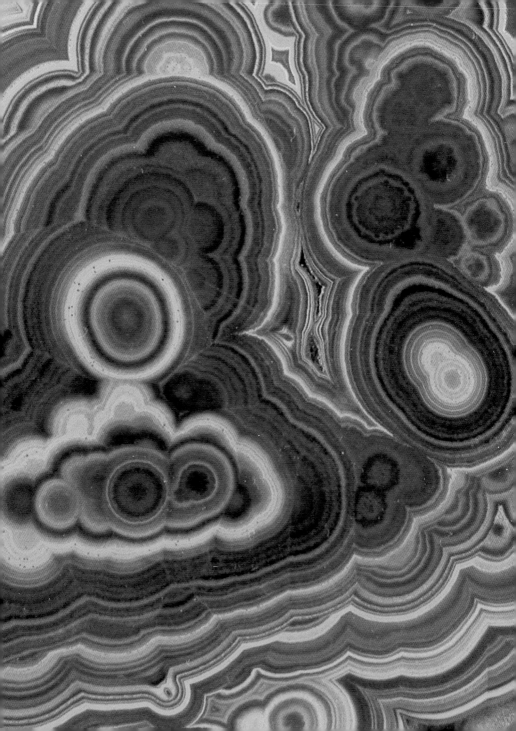

DIOPSIDE

DIOPSIDE HAS A COMFORTING, CALMING, CENTERING ENERGY THAT
CONNECTS YOU TO MOTHER NATURE AND THE FAIRY REALM.

**CHAKRA
PLACEMENT**
Heart (lower)

SPIRIT GUIDE
Archangel
Assiel

BIRTHSTONE
August

APPEARANCE

Diopside is green to dark green or black. It is transparent
to translucent.

HEALING

Diopside is soothing to the emotional body, and assists you in
feeling more centered and aligned. It is excellent for stress
relief and relaxation, especially after prolonged exertion.

It is a good all-around healing tool, and is a favorite stone
of crystal healers because of its restorative properties.
It reduces deeply entrenched stress and is useful as a
"tonic" after chronic illness.

Physically it is used to treat heart and lungs because of its
regenerative properties. Diopside also eases chronic asthma,
emphysema, bronchitis, trauma, anxiety, tension, fatigue,
and stress. Emotionally renewing, it expands the love energy
to see the beauty of the natural world.

MOLDAVITE

MOLDAVITE IS TRANSFORMATIONAL, BRINGING RAPID SPIRITUAL
EVOLUTION. IT MERGES COSMIC AND EARTHLY ENERGIES.

CHAKRA PLACEMENT
Heart (lower)

SPIRIT GUIDE
Archangel
Raphael

BIRTHSTONE
April

APPEARANCE

Moldavite is an olive green or dull greenish vitreous substance. It can be transparent or translucent mossy green, with swirls and bubbles enhancing its mossy appearance.

HEALING

Moldavite has an immediate influence on those who can attune to its energies. Moldavite has no structure; this means it can take you beyond your self-limiting belief system into uncharted realms of infinite possibilities.

•

Moldavite amplifies the energy of other stones and can be used on any chakra to facilitate the opening and cleansing process of chakra activation. Moldavite simply burns away energy blocks, expanding and transforming as it does so.

•

Moldavite strengthens the immune system, and is used as a diagnostic tool by crystal therapists to identify the roots of imbalance or disease.

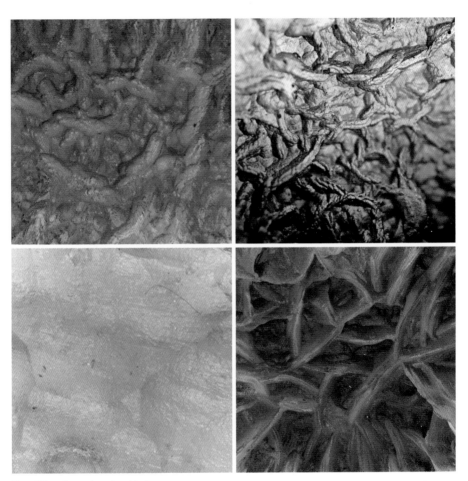

Four different samples of moldavite.

GREEN TOURMALINE

GREEN TOURMALINE BRINGS HEALING AND WHOLENESS. IT IS DEEPLY
NURTURING AND RESTORATIVE, AND IS BENEFICIAL TO ALL LIVING THINGS.

**CHAKRA
PLACEMENT**
Heart (lower)

SPIRIT GUIDE
Archangel
Raphael

BIRTHSTONE
May

APPEARANCE

Green tourmaline, also known as verdelite, ranges from
transparent to opaque.

HEALING

Green tourmaline seems to be prized above all other stones
by crystal therapists. It is also one of the premier stones for
self-healing. Green tourmaline quiets on overactive mind and
increases self-confidence, giving us a sense of belonging
and security.

•

It is used to boost the immune system and realign bones
and strained muscle tissue. It is calming to the nerves,
aids sleep, and regenerates the heart and thymus. It has
been helpful when used to combat deep-seated phobias,
especially claustrophobia and panic attacks.

•

Green tourmaline makes an excellent spring tonic at any
time of year. It is also used to calm hyperactive children.

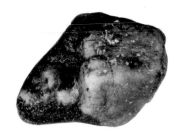

EMERALD

EMERALD IS A STONE OF HEAVENLY HARMONY. IT ENCOURAGES
PEACEFUL GROWTH, SUCCESS, AND ABUNDANCE.

CHAKRA PLACEMENT
Heart (lower)

SPIRIT GUIDE
Archangel
Raphael

BIRTHSTONE
May

APPEARANCE

Emeralds range in color from milky grass-green to the
richest transparent green.

HEALING

Emerald is steeped in mystic lore. It embodies wisdom,
intellect, and clarity of understanding. Ancient alchemy
speaks of the "Emerald Tablet," which is inscribed with
the sacred formula for enlightenment.

•

Emerald has always been associated with prophecy and
foresight as well as balance, love, and friendship. It carries
the purest ray of healing; this emerald ray balances the
heart chakra, so is used to help the related organs of the
lungs and heart.

•

Emerald helps dispel negative emotions such as rage,
scarcity, jealousy, and hatred; it works on the thymus gland,
and lowers blood pressure. It is beneficial to those who
suffer from claustrophobia because it brings gentle balance
and calm.

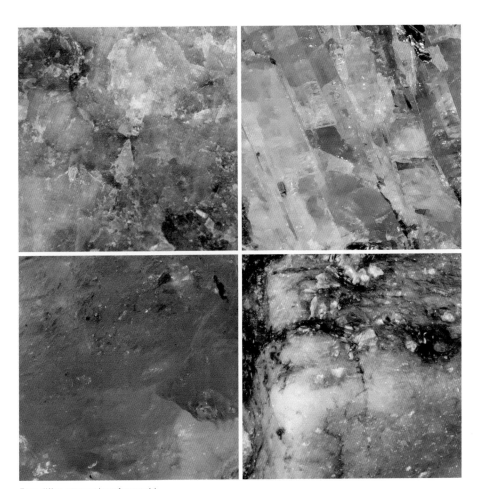

Four different samples of emerald.

MOSS AĢATE

MOSS AGATE'S ATTRIBUTES ARE ONES OF STABILITY, STRENGTH, PERSISTENCE, PERSEVERANCE, AND GROUNDING.

CHAKRA PLACEMENT
Heart (lower)

SPIRIT GUIDE
Archangel Raphael

BIRTHSTONE
May

APPEARANCE

Moss agate is translucent chalcedony with inclusions of green minerals that give it a tree-like (dendritic) appearance.

HEALING

Moss agate is beneficial to almost everyone because it contains the energy (resonance) of the earth; it is slow-acting, solid, grounded, feminine, and stable. It truly is a wonderful healing stone to use in any situation where the element of earth is needed, as it reconnects you back to the earth, bringing stability to all levels of the situation.

•

The energy of moss agate has the power of materialization and encompasses all activities of productivity, fertility, growth, and regeneration.

•

It will help support the immune system by activating the healing and balancing energies of the heart chakra. Animals and plants thrive in moss agate's energy field.

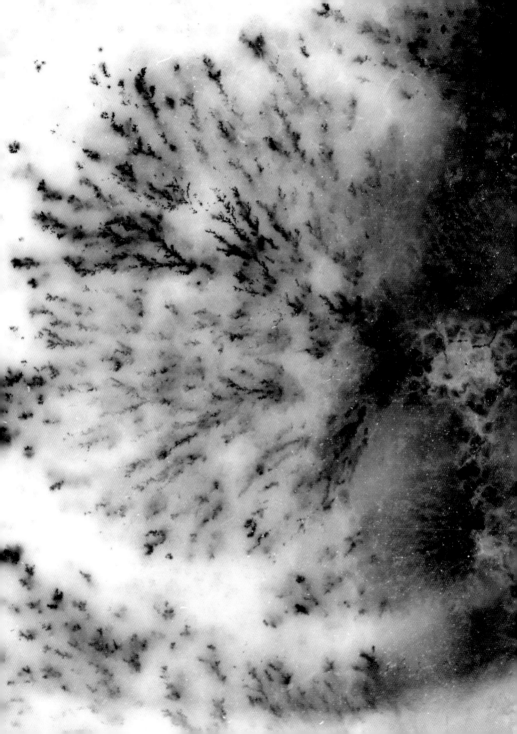

AMBER

AMBER SYMBOLIZES LIFE ENERGY. IT WAS PRIZED BY THE ANCIENTS AND HAS BEEN FASHIONED INTO JEWELRY FOR THOUSANDS OF YEARS.

CHAKRA PLACEMENT
Solar plexus

SPIRIT GUIDE
Archangel Tahariel

BIRTHSTONE
May

APPEARANCE

Amber is a time-hardened resin, ranging from yellow to brown or reddish brown. It has no crystalline structure.

HEALING

Amber works by filling gaps and holes within the auric shell that may be caused by illness, accident, surgery, stress, trauma, depression, or medication.

It swiftly infuses the aura with golden light, which invigorates the body's many systems. Amber boosts energy levels and generates joyful enthusiasm.

It is particularly useful for bringing warmth to the body, especially the hands and feet. When used in crystal therapy, it has a direct effect on the brain and nervous system. Amber allows the body to heal itself, by absorbing and transmuting negative into positive, which stimulates the metabolism.

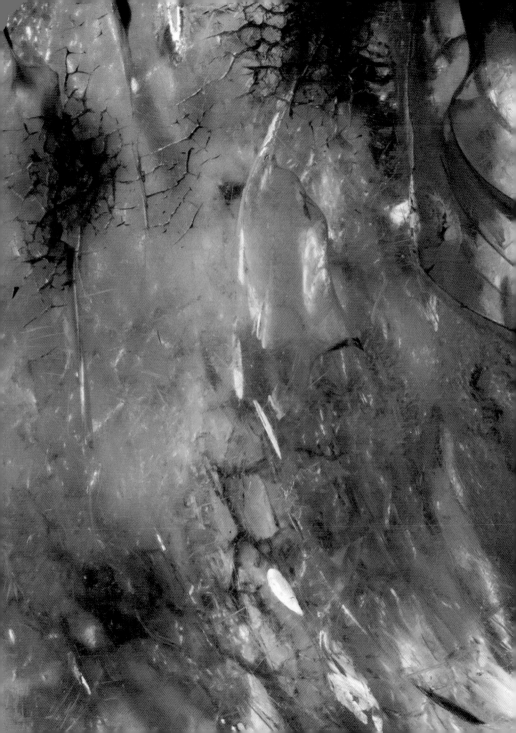

CITRINE

CITRINE QUARTZ BOOST CONFIDENCE AND
INCREASES PERSONAL POWER.

CHAKRA PLACEMENT
Solar plexus

SPIRIT GUIDE
Archangel
Jophiel

BIRTHSTONE
June

APPEARANCE

Citrine quartz has warm, sunny yellow transparent tones
with a milky white base.

HEALING

Citrine quartz is a lustrous gem of a stone that holds the key
to a balanced solar plexus chakra. This chakra is also known
as the power chakra. When it is balanced you will show
the following characteristics: spontaneity, positive mental
attitude, joy, hope, freedom from emotional hang-ups
and inhibitions, a keen thirst for knowledge, wisdom,
and spiritual understanding.

•

Citrine quartz banishes negativity, depression, and deep
sadness. It is the best crystal to use to stop energy drain.
It has been called the merchant's stone as it is believed
to attract abundance and prosperity.

•

Physically it works on the pancreas, and then all other
organs associated with the solar plexus chakra: liver,
gall bladder, spleen, and middle stomach.

RUTILE QUARTZ

RUTILE QUARTZ AMPLIFIES YOUR INTENTIONS, EXPANDS AWARENESS,
AND ACCELERATES SPIRITUAL GROWTH.

CHAKRA PLACEMENT
Solar plexus

SPIRIT GUIDE
Archangel
Melchizedeck

BIRTHSTONE
October

APPEARANCE

Rutile quartz is clear with fine strands of yellow or orange-gold, needle-like inclusions of rutile.

HEALING

Rutile quartz is uplifting and energizing; it diminishes fears and eases loneliness and depression. Rutile quartz is inspirational; it relieves feelings of guilt or shame.

•

It is an extremely protective stone that deflects outside negative energies and unwanted psychic intrusion, and for this reason it is used by mediums.

•

It swiftly clears pathways; this will aid and speed up healing, so it is an extremely useful crystal. It also helps repair damaged tissue, broken bones, and torn muscles. When placed on the solar plexus chakra, rutile quartz aids the absorption of nutrients to promote general good health. Mentally it stimulates creativity, helping you to manifest your goals and move your life toward abundance and prosperity.

108

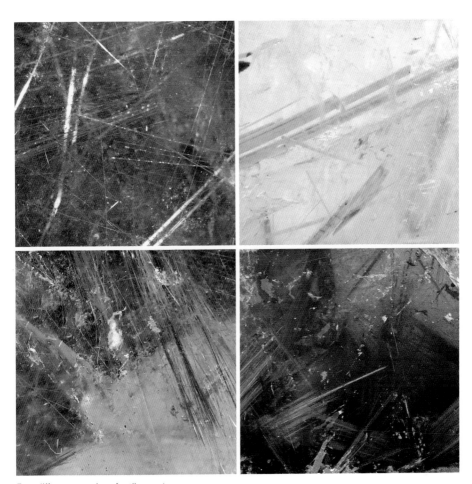

Four different samples of rutile quartz.

TIGER'S EYE

TIGER'S EYE AIDS CLARITY OF PERCEPTION, GIVING INSIGHT
INTO IMBALANCES THAT HAVE BLOCKED CREATIVITY.

CHAKRA PLACEMENT
Solar plexus

SPIRIT GUIDE
Archangel
Verchiel

BIRTHSTONE
June

APPEARANCE

Tiger's eye has bands of yellow-brown to golden colors and
exhibits chatoyancy.

HEALING

Like all stones that resemble eyes when cut and polished,
tiger's eye is used as a protective amulet against the
"evil eye."

Tiger's eye deals with issues of low self-worth and lack of
personal creativity. It releases stuck or congested energy
when placed on the solar plexus chakra. It allows you to see
your own faults and understand different perspectives, which
means it can bring harmony to families and relationships
where differences of opinion or expression are causing
discord. Tiger's eye helps you to find balance through
resolving inner and outer conflict.

Physically it is fortifying, supporting general vitality. It is
strengthening to the endocrine system, bringing stability
to the hormonal system.

YELLOW TOPAZ

TOPAZ IS REVITALIZING AND ENLIVENING. IT IS VALUED
FOR ITS MANIFESTING PROPERTIES.

**CHAKRA
PLACEMENT**
Solar plexus

SPIRIT GUIDE
Archangel
Jophiel

BIRTHSTONE
November

APPEARANCE

Yellow topaz (or imperial topaz) is a transparent gemstone.

HEALING

Topaz contains exceptionally beneficial energies. It is
revitalizing to the mental body, bringing feelings of vitality
and exceptional well-being. A magnificent natural, long topaz
crystal makes a marvellous healing wand that is able to
focus huge amounts of healing energy into the solar plexus
chakra to enliven the whole body and aura.

•

It is often used to treat gall bladder, spleen, and stomach
disorders, as well as problems with the pancreas and liver.
When used in healing it helps us release pent-up tensions,
including anger, resentment, bitterness, and other negative
emotions, so it should be used wisely and with caution.

•

It is a powerful gemstone and, when used in meditation,
brings personal power and self-mastery.

CARNELIAN

CARNELIAN HAS A LONG HISTORY OF USE IN VEDIC ASTROLOGY. IT IS WORN
AS AN AMULET FOR COURAGE, CONFIDENCE, AND PROTECTION.

CHAKRA PLACEMENT
Sacral

SPIRIT GUIDE
Archangel
Ariel

BIRTHSTONE
April

APPEARANCE

Carnelian ranges from pale orange to orangey red. It is
densely colored opaque to translucent.

HEALING

Carnelian's energy signature is strong, stimulating, and
creative. When used in crystal healing it has the potential
to balance the sacral chakra.

•

Carnelian can help to ground thoughts and emotions. It has
been used to protect the user from hatred, envy, and rage.
It also lifts the spirits by banishing negativity.

•

For those who suffer from existential fears, past physical
or emotional abuse, vitality-sapping illnesses, or any long-
standing mental anguish, carnelian is a good ongoing
supplement to their life force and should be carried or
worn as a pendant or ring on a regular basis.

COPPER

COPPER WAS SACRED TO VENUS, THE ROMAN GODDESS
OF LOVE, BEAUTY, AND CREATIVITY.

**CHAKRA
PLACEMENT**
Sacral

SPIRIT GUIDE
Archangel
Chamuel

BIRTHSTONE
April

APPEARANCE

Copper forms in nuggets that can be smooth or dendritic.
Green copper oxides may be present.

HEALING

Wearing copper in the form of a bracelet is well known as a
folklore remedy for reducing the aches and pains of arthritis
and rheumatism.

•

The frequency of copper resonates with the sacral chakra,
stimulating regenerative and healing capabilities. It connects
you to primal creative energy, giving you the courage to give
birth to your dreams. It is excellent when used in meditation
because it guides you deep within yourself to discover what
you need to move forward on your journey.

•

Physically it is anti-inflammatory and soothing, and reduces
stiffness in muscles and joints. Emotionally it eases
emotional tension and creative frustration.

GARNET

GARNET PROVIDES FORTITUDE, STRENGTH, AND SECURITY.
IT ASSISTS YOU IN MANIFESTING YOUR DREAMS.

**CHAKRA
PLACEMENT**
Root

SPIRIT GUIDE
Archangel
Uriel

BIRTHSTONE
January

APPEARANCE

Almandine garnet is red and transparent to translucent.

HEALING

Almandine garnet contains the energy of courage, endurance, perseverance, tenacity, forbearance, vigor, fortitude, stamina, and self-mastery. These qualities are all the signs of a balanced root chakra.

•

Garnets keep you grounded and solidly anchored to the earth, bringing a feeling of vigorous good health and boundless vitality. They help you to understand the energy of gravity, allowing you to connect to the vastness of the earth's energy grid. When you are fully "earthed," nothing can shake you. Without a strong foundation you will not be able to grow to your full potential and succeed in life.

•

Garnets are used for psychic protection because, when you have a strong root chakra, you are less open to the negative influences of other people.

RED JASPER

RED JASPER IS AN EARTHY GROUNDING STONE THAT IS
ENERGIZING, BRINGING STRENGTH AND VITALITY.

CHAKRA PLACEMENT
Root

SPIRIT GUIDE
Archangel
Ariel

BIRTHSTONE
April

APPEARANCE

Red jasper is opaque and red-brown.

HEALING

Red jasper is a slow, steady, reliable healing stone that works to increase stamina and endurance. It strengthens the root chakra and reinforces your connection to the earth. Such a connection can improve your overall health and sense of emotional well-being, bringing renewed enthusiasm.

Red jasper is a protective stone that encourages you to focus on practical solutions. The energy is also helpful in stressful situations when it is important to retain one's own boundaries.

It helps with the removal of toxins from the liver and large intestine. It will support you during the releasing process by gently stabilizing your energy field, easing the discomfort normally associated with toxin release. Red jasper encourages you to take responsibility for your own emotional health.

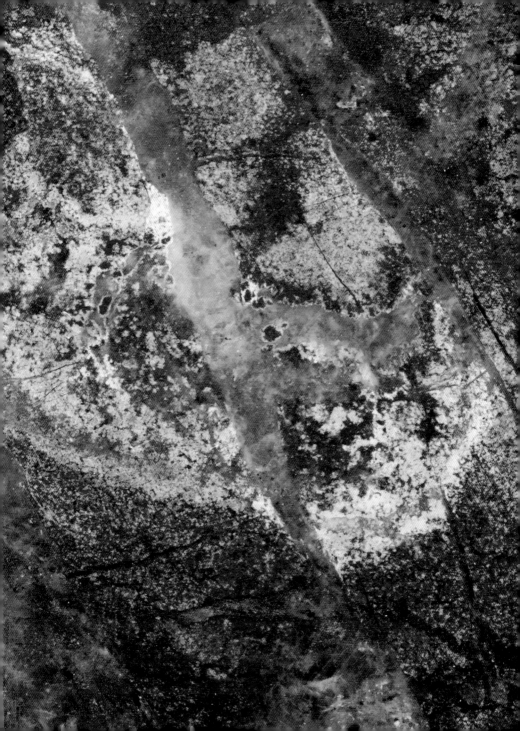

SMOKY QUARTZ

SMOKY QUARTZ HELPS TO STRENGTHEN, STABILIZE,
AND PROTECT OUR FUNDAMENTAL ENERGIES.

CHAKRA PLACEMENT
Root

SPIRIT GUIDE
Archangel
Sandalphon

BIRTHSTONE
January

APPEARANCE

Smoky quartz is light to dark brown and transparent.

HEALING

Smoky quartz is stimulating and purifying to the root chakra, so it is good for meditation practice. It brings you safely back to earth and normal, everyday, waking reality.

•

Smoky quartz aids clarity of thought, so it supports contemplation. It can help you bring your dreams into reality. It eases despair and despondency; it enhances survival instincts by neutralizing over-emotional states. It is an ideal crystal to hold or carry when you feel confused or afraid. Smoky quartz encourages the integration of disparate energies with practical focus.

•

It is also used to relieve headaches and congestion of the intestines, help heal the feet and legs, and ease lower back pain. It relieves muscular cramp. Placing smoky quartz in the environment helps prevent the unwanted accumulation of electromagnetic resonance.

OBSIDIAN

BLACK OBSIDIAN IS THE WARRIOR OF TRUTH AND USED FOR PROTECTION.
IT REPELS NEGATIVITY AND DISPELS PSYCHIC POLLUTION.

**CHAKRA
PLACEMENT**
Root

SPIRIT GUIDE
Archangel
Israfel

BIRTHSTONE
November

APPEARANCE

Obsidian is black to brownish gray. It is translucent and
glassy in appearance.

HEALING

Obsidian is a "master mineral" in the magical art of
the hidden, lost, or forbidden. It has no restrictions or
limitations. This is entirely due to its amorphous structure;
it teaches us to let go of our limitations and self-imposed
fear restrictions. It teaches us to flow and expand.

It has a soul-mirror quality that is all its own. Obsidian is
used for divination; it is traditionally polished to make scrying
tools. It is excellent at revealing the truth in all situations.

It is used for physical grounding and to rebalance the
digestive system. Pain can be eased when obsidian is placed
over the affected area. It has been used in the treatment of
arthritic and joint pain.

INDEX

CREDITS